The MSP's Guide to the Ultimate Client Experience

*Optimizing service efficiency, account
management productivity, and client engagement
with a modern digital-first approach.*

Jeff Farris

Azurative, LLC – dba CloudRadial
6060 N. Central Expressway, #500
Dallas, TX 75206
www.cloudradial.com

ISBN 978-0-578-98667-8
Library of Congress Control Number: 2021920377

About CloudRadial

For purposes of illustration, references are made to CloudRadial, the first and leading digital-first client portal for MSPs and internal IT teams. For more information about CloudRadial, visit:

https://www.cloudradial.com

At the website, you can also sign up for a demo or a free trial. Sign up for the newsletter to get on the CloudRadial mailing list.

Summary

The cloud and digital technologies have led to a dramatic overhaul of everyday life. We no longer shop, play, date and especially work like we did just twenty years ago.

When we look around, we see major big-box retailers going out of business not because they didn't have clean, well-stocked stores but because they failed to evolve a digital strategy to utilize those stores.

The process of digital transformation is remaking everything. But no one should recognize this change better than MSPs – digital transformation made the modern MSP industry. RMMs gave IT service companies the technology that turned them into SaaS providers, justifying a SaaS-like pricing model of monthly recurring revenue. MRR has shaped the industry ever since.

Digital transformation of an MSPs internal business operations is over. Nearly every MSP now uses cloud-based infrastructure for quoting, ticketing, invoicing, and integrating other cloud-based tools beyond the RMM to enhance and extend their service offerings such as backup and cloud servers.

But while MSPs have benefitted from their own internal digital transformation, most have yet to apply these changes in a way that a client directly experiences. It's as if MSPs have digitized their "store inventory," but not their "store." Clients are expected to interact with MSPs the same way they did when the industry began.

This book shows you how to transform your client experience into something truly exceptional. It shows you how a digital-first client experience completely remakes the way you can land, onboard, manage and grow clients.

Author's Note

In 1982, at the age of 23, I became the Manager of Office Automation for the Southland Corporation, the parent company of 7-Eleven. I reported to the VP of MIS. His primary concern was the company's mainframe computer and IT staff, which took two floors of our Dallas headquarters. Though my title sounded good, in reality, my initial responsibilities were for one older Apple II and two new IBM personal computers.

But my next five years were on the front lines of the personal computer revolution and a revolution it was! When I started, secretaries and IBM electric typewriters were everywhere. Executives had personal secretaries, and everyone else had a shared secretary. Memos were typed and placed in interoffice envelopes for delivery. It was still very "Mad Men" even though it was 20 years later.

When I left in 1987, the personal computer was everywhere. Typewriters had been replaced by computers, computers were connected to local area networks, and the mainframe served as backbone for electronic mail and document delivery. In those five years, the team I built, and I had to learn how to:

- Evaluate and set standards for personal computer hardware and software purchases
- Consult with departments on office automation strategies
- Approve every computer purchase
- Install new computer systems
- Conduct classroom and one-on-one training
- Provide phone and walk-in support
- Work with HR to set usage policies
- Coordinate repairs

If these duties seem familiar, it's because they are still the duties performed by managed service providers and internal IT departments. Names and vendors change, but the needs don't seem to.

We didn't implement computers because they were new; we implemented them because department managers wanted improved productivity, collaboration, and decision making. The $10,000 cost of a PC, printer, and plotter (back then, required for charts) was easily offset by the improved decision-making process that resulted. Insights that were previously hidden were now more easily seen and communicated throughout the company.

Not once did we pitch department managers on the advantage of the 386 over the 286 processor; instead, we talked their language and delivered on the transformation they needed to improve their results. The personal computer was new, and it took education to help these managers understand the transformation that was and wasn't possible with these new technologies and approaches.

Fast forward almost 40 years, and we are here at an inflection point again. The "cloud," Microsoft 365, mobility, high-speed Internet, and video are at the forefront of the next revolution in productivity, collaboration, and decision making. The debate of in-office vs. remote-work will ultimately bring even more significant changes in the economy than the personal computer did.

This coming revolution means it's a great time to be working as an MSP or in internal IT but not on the existing models. MSPs that view equipment, support, and maintenance as their expertise will become the electric typewriter repair people of the future (not good), while those facilitating the change and transformation in clients will see revenues and profitability dramatically increase (very good).

This book lays out both the foundations and real-world steps you'll take to achieve this transformation. Whether external, internal, or working in co-managed roles, the issues are similar; it's just the number of clients you support. Internal supports one, external supports many. Going forward, I'll use the term managed service provider, or MSP, that is meant to cover any of these approaches.

I hope you find value in this guide.

Jeff Farris

Table of Contents

Table of Figures

Introduction

"But the big change is the digital acceleration. In the past, it was like, 'We have a retail strategy, and we have a digital strategy.' There is no retail strategy. The retail strategy is simply there to support your digital strategy, as opposed to vice versa. So, the acceleration of digital, and then obviously everything that goes around that, remote access, cybersecurity, all those kind of things."

Robert Herjavec -- Newsweek, December 17, 2020

Not too long ago we went to the store to consult sales staff on which TV, car, stereo, book, etc. was better, more reliable, or interesting. Retail stores were a place to explore and then a place to purchase. Now, retail is the place of pickup. It's where we go to view or pick up an item we've already researched and most likely purchased online. Every retailer is becoming an Amazon, and every retail store just a fitting room, showroom, or warehouse.

This digital transformation isn't just about brick-and-mortar businesses. In fact, digital transformation has been the foundation of the entire MSP industry. Remote management and monitoring tools, RMMs, made IT service companies into SaaS providers justifying SaaS-like pricing with a monthly recurring revenue model. MRR has made the industry what it is today.

The digital transformation of an MSPs back-office operations is complete. Almost every MSP uses cloud-based infrastructure for quoting, ticketing, invoicing, and integrates other cloud-based tools beyond the RMM to enhance and extend their service offerings.

Transitioning from Labor to Outcomes

As more client technology has shifted to the cloud, and just like the MSP, most clients are also undergoing or have undergone a digital transformation. The client's cloud infrastructure is forcing MSPs to switch from a labor-centric approach to solving problems to an outcomes-focused approach. In other words, it has become less about going onsite to fix a problem and more about making sure the correct systems are selected, implemented, automated, and monitored. These processes ensure that problems either don't happen or are fixed with minimal effort.

Described another way, MSPs used to help clients directly. But this help is becoming indirect. Now MSPs "help" technology that helps and manages clients. MSPs no longer worry about swapping backup tapes and instead worry about making sure the backup systems run as set up in their configurations.

Implementing Security – The Canary in the Coal Mine

Just like canaries warned miners of dangers, security issues are forcing every MSP to start thinking about an outcomes-based business model. Clients don't care how many hours it takes to install or manage security; they just don't want any problems. Low-cost and low-labor solutions don't define success. Only no problems define success.

Unfortunately, many managed service contracts are built around determining labor costs and stack costs to define a per endpoint or per user pricing model. These cost-plus agreements don't value the outcomes clients are now expecting. Service tickets, which were often a measure of MSP productivity, no longer tell an accurate story. If you get only one ticket and the subject is "Can't access data – ransomware," it doesn't matter how smoothly everything else runs.

But a smooth-running MSP that generates successful daily outcomes shouldn't generate a lot of tickets. But if clients don't generate tickets, how will they know that they need the MSP?

Keeping the Lights On

Few of us spend much time looking at our electric bills. Electric companies charge us monthly for the electricity we use, and we seldom quarrel with the charges. Why? Because every day, we saw the lights on and knew they were doing their job.

Compare this to an MSPs monthly bill, and you'll see the frustration many clients face when it comes time to pay. The cloud has made much of the MSP's job transparent to users but not less essential. Often, MSPs send their own internal reports to clients to show them the efforts they undertook. But that is like the electric company trying to explain transformers and line voltages to us. Clients know their MSPs care about those things, but why should they?

Compounding this problem is the typical QBR or business review. Because clients can start questioning their MSP relationship, the QBR becomes a perpetual resell exercise reviewing technical data or stack alignments that quickly loses a client's interest.

The shift to an outcomes-focused model is not well supported by traditional client experiences, which typically follows this path:

1. MSP finds prospect and convinces prospect that they are capable, trustworthy, and reliable.
2. Prospect becomes a client.
3. Client is told to ask for help anytime they need it. Sometimes, the MSP even makes it easier to ask for help with a tray icon or desktop button.
4. MSP does the work, and then prints or emails reports to show the client their efforts.
5. MSP and client talk regularly/sometimes/never to talk about "things."
6. Sometimes these "things" are simply the MSP reminding the client how capable, trustworthy, and reliable they are, and the process starts again at step 1.

To bring digital transformation to the client relationship, MSPs must think and deliver different. They must think from the customer back to their own business, and then show the clients they have "kept the lights on" every single day.

Delivering a Digital-First Client Experience

Think about Amazon or almost any shopping site. These sites aren't places you go to buy; they are places you go to search, dream, research, and even sometimes purchase. Early online sites were about inventory (the retailer's problems), the successful sites were about all these other services (the consumer's problems).

To deliver a digital-first experience, you'll need your own SaaS like portal where clients can go to engage with your services. It shouldn't be a place people visit just to solve a problem or track ticket "inventory"; it should be an extension of what people do with their technology and how they interact with you. Just like Amazon, the portal should be a place where clients learn, engage, find ideas, and even purchase.

A portal isn't just about ticketing. Even if clients never need to submit or review a ticket, the portal should be a place that they find helpful in their daily work. Ideally, the portal will be perceived as their portal with the ability to customize and adapt it to their own unique needs. A good portal makes every client feel like they are being serviced by a "boutique" provider who truly understands their issues – no matter the size of your operation.

Because CloudRadial was the first product on the market to address this integrated and comprehensive approach for clients, I'll focus on using CloudRadial to deliver this digital-first approach to redefining the four key steps of the client relationship:

1. <u>Landing</u> – Delivering a sales presentation focusing on the value you'll be delivering daily to your prospect.
2. <u>Onboarding</u> – Taking on a new client and familiarizing them with your services and processes.
3. <u>Managing</u> – Keeping clients up to date with new information and handling service requests.
4. <u>Growing</u> – Creating new ways to engage with clients and redefining the QBR in the process.

The next few chapters will cover these topics with actual steps to help you create the ultimate client experience.

Landing Clients

If you ask managed service providers or their clients what a managed services provider does, the answer will generally fall into one big category "helps with technology." This umbrella statement covers one-man MSPs working out of their house all the way to IBM helping Fortune 500 companies. "Helps with technology" offers a low barrier of entry that anyone can jump.

However, that low barrier entry also has a much higher cost of success. While it's true that anyone can help, not everyone can demonstrate the same level of value when it comes to the complexities of using technology to deliver business growth.

In the sales process, your challenge is to overcome the "IT is a commodity" mindset many clients start with. You need to show that choosing the right firm is even more important than finding the right law firm or accountant because IT is something that will affect them every single day.

Selling Risk Has Problems

No potential client ever started their business to buy IT services. IT services may be the lifeblood of their business, but in almost every case it won't be their business. Like other professional services, potential clients need the best provider but often lack the means to determine between two proposals. In these situations, personality, trust, or referrals (conveyed trust) have been essential. To demonstrate competence, the sales process often includes assessments and resulting technical reports that use terms that clients don't understand and often includes lots of "red" warnings that clients will hopefully want resolved.

This sales approach is effective and is often a great way to get a client appointment, but it starts the relationship focused on risk reduction rather than partnership. After the reports show "green" the risks are gone (at least from the client's perspective), and clients may start to question the continued high monthly fees. Think of it from a client's other experiences – after a lawyer provides them an agreement, they don't keep charging a monthly fee, so why are you?

Stop Selling Trust, Start Selling Outcomes

Before we can transform how you land a client, you need to take a good, hard look at what you've been selling. Generally speaking, the biggest issue behind the MSP sales approach is that it has been about trust.

We can boil down the sales conversation to something like this:

- Trust that we're using the best tools.
- Trust that we're the right people for the job.
- Trust that we know what we're talking about.
- Trust that we'll do a better job than the other guy.
- Other people trust us.

The big issue with the trust approach is that anyone can make these promises. The bigger issue is why should trust be a factor or even the determining factor? Clients don't really trust anyone. They expect banks to send them statements, electric companies to send them usage details and even employees must prove that they accomplished the goals set out for them. So why sell trust if clients aren't comfortable with that concept? Especially, if you can't follow through with proving you've done your job!

And, since many MSPs use the same tools in their stack, there's no easy way for a prospect to know who the best choice is for a good partnership.

How can you break free of this never-ending battle to be more believable than the other guy?

Here's the simple answer: Don't lead with trust.

Instead, prove to the prospect that you're different from the very first meeting. With a digital-first approach, you've got a way to do that every single day, starting from that very first meeting.

Starting on the Right Foundation

With a digital foundation, the relationship can start on a different path. Instead of just focusing on risk and trust, the original sales proposition can focus on giving the client things that they will value:

- Increased transparency and control
- Easier IT access
- Improved productivity
- Enhanced compliance
- Ongoing planning
- More business efficiency and opportunity

Now rather than the sales effort being about solving one problem, the relationship starts as a partnership that will evolve to meet new IT challenges. This relationship is more likely to result in you becoming their vCIO rather than their break/fix IT department.

This vCIO approach then sets the stage for more collaborative client engagement which has gone from a "nice-to-have" to "must have" approach. Whether it is security, cloud infrastructure, Microsoft Office deployments, productivity, or especially planning for changes, it is impossible to do any of these without active client participation.

The cloud has placed limits on the ability of MSPs to protect clients and create efficient infrastructure without engaging, training, and monitoring user efforts. And it is no longer enough to work with just the primary decision-makers in an organization. Shadow IT, the usage of cloud applications without a business owners' approval, can be initiated by anyone in the client company and creates additional IT responsibilities whether you know they are there or not.

Defining the Sales Process

So, let's explore what an evolved sales approach might look like. With a little bit of effort, let's tweak your sales process in a way that makes your prospect meetings much more likely to turn into client onboardings.

To land a new client, most MSPs follow a sales process that boils down to three key phases and often three meetings:

- Learning
- Assessing
- Presenting

Each phase has different goals, both for you and the client. Let's explore each in depth.

Conducting the First Meeting – Learning

Core Objective
- Build a base understanding with the prospective client.

Action Steps
- Listen to the prospect.

Most of the first meeting with a prospect is simply listening to them and adequately understanding their needs. Let the prospect tell you everything they're willing to share about their business operations, their current IT processes, their pain points, and more. The most important and primary question to ask is:

- Why are they giving you time to discuss their IT needs?

Time is the most valuable commodity most people have and understanding how you got the meeting will be critical to creating a winning proposal. Beyond this question, some of the other things you'll want to understand include:

- What problems does their business solve for their clients?
- Who are their clients?
- How do they interact with clients?
- Who are their employees?
- Which employees are part of the executive team?
- Where do their employees work?
- How often are employees mobile or working from home?
- How have they grown in the past?
- How do they expect to grow in the future?
- How has Covid impacted their business?
- What activities do they do every day? On a regular basis?
- How is technology used in these activities?
- Where is the technology located? Cloud? Closet?
- What is required in their industry in case they have a ransomware attack?

- Who setup, maintains, or trains on the current technology?
- What keeps the executive team up at night?

Keep all these things in mind (and preferably written down). You'll want to share these details with your team to come up with a compelling solution that addresses their primary question.

Laying Down an IT Foundation

Take the prospect's needs to heart. From the very first conversation with them, make sure you paint a clear picture of how you'd help drive their business growth as their IT partner.

Sell yourself as a strategic IT business partner rather than the IT handyman. Your suggestions and implemented solutions can directly benefit the client to help them make money, save money, and reduce their operational risk. As a business owner, that's a million times better than someone who just fixes issues.

But before you can deliver on that, you must set the expectation of building an IT foundation based on:

- Improving client control
- Enhancing client productivity

With it, you can build a long-term game plan that shows the prospect what a tangible path to growth looks like. Without it, you're stuck in a loop of performing one-off projects or flat-rate monthly fees.

The following diagram shows our suggested hierarchy of business needs to build your foundation.

As each part of the foundation becomes more stable, you can move on to the next one above, which lets you have a more significant and effective impact on business operations. The higher up on the hierarchy you go, the higher the value you deliver to clients and the higher margins you can achieve with products and services that deliver real outcomes.

Lower levels can be viewed by clients as commodities and become price sensitive for these solutions. Upper levels solve real client problems with a positive impact to overall operations.

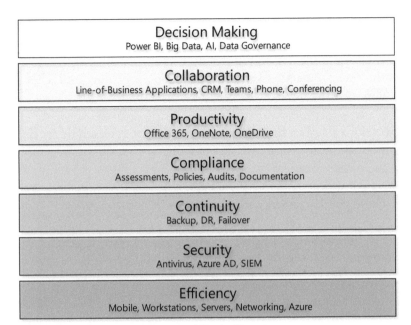

| Decision Making |
| Power BI, Big Data, AI, Data Governance |

| Collaboration |
| Line-of-Business Applications, CRM, Teams, Phone, Conferencing |

| Productivity |
| Office 365, OneNote, OneDrive |

| Compliance |
| Assessments, Policies, Audits, Documentation |

| Continuity |
| Backup, DR, Failover |

| Security |
| Antivirus, Azure AD, SIEM |

| Efficiency |
| Mobile, Workstations, Servers, Networking, Azure |

Figure 1 - IT Value Hierarchy

Taking care of the simpler day-to-day activities like workstation support builds the business's core on efficiency. Once that's stable, you can start to lay down security. Then, continuity – and so on.

Demonstrating Daily Transparency

Let's cut the theory for a second. Let's talk about what CloudRadial[1] has to do with this.

CloudRadial is a digital-first client portal that consolidates all your client interactions in one place. With CloudRadial, you've got the platform to show the client exactly what this foundation looks like. From day-to-day ticketing to report archiving, you've got the means to give them a way to see all the efforts coming to fruition on-demand, online, and from any device.

And let's face it – that's a must-have in the modern era, especially for IT organizations. It doesn't make any sense to talk about creating a modern approach for clients if you can't deliver on that promise. As the first and most comprehensive solution, CloudRadial is the best way to show how digital transformation can be applied to your clients.

---

[1] Get a demo or trial of CloudRadial at https://www.cloudradial.com.

The other side of the coin here is that it's not just a show-and-tell platform. A shared portal is going to give the client as much say as you in the process. Turning your relationship into a transparent, actionable, and collaborative plan lets the client understand what you're doing for them (and where you're taking them) every single day.

But there's not a need to show them everything, or even anything, during the first meeting. Remember, the first meeting is about listening, but it will be tempting to get ahead of the process because you'll see how much you can help. A good process and patience are required to let the clients catch up with where you know you can take them.

After you've gotten the first expectations out of the way, it's time to show them what this process looks like and how you'll potentially be working with them from now on.

Let's get to work on preparing for the assessment phase.

Section Recap

- Come prepared with questions to ask the prospect about their business.
- Leave a flyer showing your approach to the IT foundation.

Conducting the Second Meeting – Assessment

Core Objective

- Gauge the client as a prospective partner while also getting details on their environment.

Action Steps

- Examine the prospect's current situation and determine their viability as a client

There's no faster way to lose money than to sign a contract with a company that's a bad fit.

The first few meetings with the prospect are just as important for you as they are for them – take great care to note any red flags that the prospect may show during any of your meetings with them.

These flags may include, but aren't limited to:

- Unnecessarily badmouthing their current (or ex) IT services provider.
- Complaining of attempts at nickel and diming – especially when their infrastructure is outdated.
- Having too great a mess of a current IT infrastructure (that you'd be on the hook for when things go wrong).
- Insisting on a reactive approach and unwillingness to work towards becoming proactive.

Unfortunately, it's not always easy to catch these types of clients before signing on with them.

But if you can spot troubled clients before you're tied to them, it's certainly worth weeding them out at this stage before experiencing the pain firsthand.

One thing that shouldn't be a disqualifier is a negative or difficult member of the client's team. If the client has had previous bad experiences, you'll need to make it your mission to show them how your approach and results are different. You will win them over by giving them an early proof-of-concept that lets them see for themselves.

Creating a Proof of Concept

If they pass the first test, you'll start off by creating a company for them in CloudRadial itself with just their name. Assign a generalized feature set to them, as well as some general company groups. These features let you customize the portal to specific client needs so that every client has a custom portal. In fact, each client will have at least two different versions of the portal – one for the company administrative staff and another for the end-users.

The goal here is to build a mock-up so that you can help the prospect envision what it'll be like to work collaboratively with you as you work to grow their business. You'll be filling their company out with information as you progress through this assessment phase.

Filling Out the Proof of Concept

Now, you'll want to gather data from the client and turn it around to show them how you'd improve their organization. What's the best way to go about that?

One way would be to run an assessment against their organization – this can be as simple or as complex as you need. In CloudRadial, you can have this assessment set within their company as something you can present to them later.

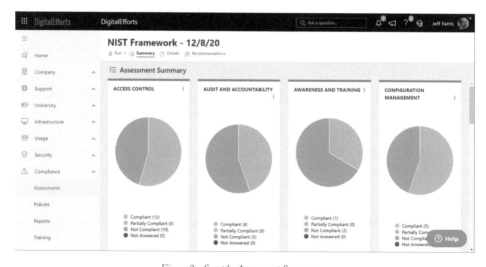

Figure 2 - Sample Assessment Summary

Aside from manual assessments, many MSPs also run discovery tools to generate reports on prospective client's environments.

If most of the current MSP tools on the market are to be believed, the approach is to show up to a prospect's place of business, run a report (or several) on their infrastructure, show it to the client and call it a day.

When the report inevitably spits out some trouble spots – like potential security issues, network conflicts, warranty expirations, etc. – it'll highlight them in red and give the MSP something to put back into the client's hands. These reports can be incredibly useful but be cautious – there are some massive drawbacks to them.

- It sets your relationship with the prospective client as transactional.

  Right off the bat, you're setting the expectation that all of the nitty-gritty aspects of IT should be "green" across the board rather than focusing on the bigger picture of business operations. The next time someone else comes along and runs an assessment against you, you'll look bad – especially if they find some red.

- It might make you look unappealing against the current IT provider.

  Changing IT providers can be very painful. If the reports come back with not much red on them, you're instantly out of the running as a new partner. The more you rely on the "fix the red" approach, the more you're susceptible to this happening to you.

- It makes shopping for the lowest bidder much easier.

  The last glaring flaw from the print-and-present approach to assessing a client is that they have zero obligation to choose you. Anyone can run a report, even with the same tool. Who's to say that the client decides to work with you? Without painting a bigger picture, you've just rattled off a laundry list of to-dos that anyone can take care of.

While these reports DO have inherent value, they shouldn't stand on their own. To beat the drawbacks, you need to sell yourself as the vCIO that drives the strategy around them.

Frame the findings in a way that builds you up as an expert on the IT foundation.

If significant issues are found with the staff's endpoints, you've got core efficiency issues to resolve before moving on to higher-level objectives (like improving overall collaboration or productivity).

Conversely, if things are stable and green in key areas, you can build a plan around the next steps regarding improving strategy, security, compliance, and more.

CloudRadial's data gathering agent is designed to capture specific bits of information from endpoints and servers and frame them in foundational terms so that you'll have a much easier time making yourself transparent to your clients.

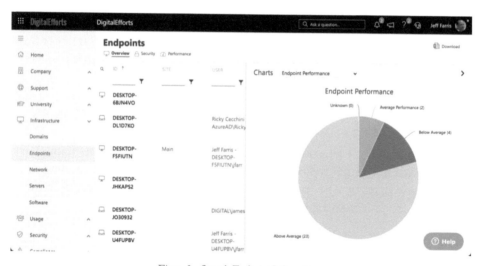

Figure 3 - Sample Endpoint Information

If possible, deploy out the agent on the client's environment and set up your policies to show them how you'll be visualizing these objectives throughout their engagement with you.

Gathering and Streamlining Assessment Results

Once you've gotten the core information gathering done, you'll want to bring all of the information together in CloudRadial to really sell yourself to the client.

Before you meet with them to discuss the results, ask yourself:

- How can you make it easy for a client to access and understand these reports?
- What are the most significant areas of opportunity to tackle that will change their business?
- Where do you start with building a plan to help them ultimately make money, save money, and reduce risk?

Don't forget that CloudRadial doesn't have to exist in a bubble. Between the assessments and agent data, there's always room for any other reports or bits of information that you think add to the conversation.

Remember to establish yourself and your portal as a central, reliable hub of information. Forward any report to a report archive within that client's company to keep everything in one spot.

Once you've gathered all the necessary data, you're ready to present your findings to the prospect.

Section Recap

- Set up the prospect's company in your CloudRadial tenant.
- Run them through a new client assessment.
- Configure policies.
- Deploy CloudRadial data agent on as many workstations, and servers as the client will allow.
- Forward any other assessment tool into CloudRadial and show them the report archive function.

Conducting the Third Meeting – Presentation

Core Objective

- Bring tool reports, assessments, and your recommendations together to show the client what it looks like to work with you every single day.

Action Steps

- Paint a picture of what it's like to work with a great IT partner.

When you meet back with the prospect, it'll be time to show them the results of what you found during the assessment phase. Remember to keep everything in context of the greater IT foundation to build that expectation of making money, saving money, and reducing risk.

The presentation itself is your own private-labeled CloudRadial instance – specifically, within their individual company. Walk them through your findings from the assessment(s), policies, and any additional reports from the report archives.

Figure 4 - Sample Portal Home Page

Remember that the portal is your service and you're showing them a glimpse of what it's like to work with you as a partner. Make it clear to them that these things are accessible 24/7 from any device, along with hundreds of other pieces of data, all on-demand.

And it's not just the big picture stuff for reporting, either.

This is the time to really embellish on your superior client experience for all their users. Show them how the portal will give their entire organization customizable access to a ton of features, like:

- Online ticketing and ticket history.
- A service catalog for things they can order from you.
- End-user training and completion tracking.
- Customizable documentation.
- Messaging/banners to always keep them up to date.

To drive the point home and summarize the conversation, you'll turn your attention to the planner.

Showing a Plan for a Client's Growth

You need to drive home the fact that you're not just going to be capturing data for fun. You'll also be sharing it with them like an open book.

The reports and assessments are your way of showing them that you're doing the work and keeping an eye on the critical stuff, but the planner is where the roadmap and suggestions get built out.

Figure 5 - Sample Planner

During the meeting, the discussion should end on the planner piece of CloudRadial. Here, you'll want to prepare some simplified services in the form of planner cards to visually showcase the plan of action for the prospect.

Set the expectation from the beginning that you'll need their collaboration regularly so that you can help keep them aligned to their more important foundational goals.

Your goal is to show the client that you're matching your services and solutions to their needs with the IT foundation in mind. It's why we have the foundational categories (Efficiency, Security, Continuity, etc.) appended to every single planner card – that helps keep every single conversation grounded in the bigger picture.

Once you paint the picture of the path to success with the planner, your meeting is complete. You've now met with the prospect, assessed their needs, stored all the data in neat siloes within CloudRadial, and given them an action plan to move forward with. In practice, the planner will be your "yes" board where you'll present recommendations to clients and get approvals for implementation.

If you have at least one email address from the prospect's side, you can even give them a link to access the data you gathered within their CloudRadial company. That's a powerful leave-behind to show them all the work you've done is as good as theirs.

Section Recap

- Use the portal as a leave-behind for the client.
- Use the planner to set the expectation of service to implement.

Delivering Better Sales Process

When you put it all together, you end up with something special.
You no longer must rely on the "trust me" approach and hope that
prospects believe you. With a digital-first approach, you can walk into a
prospect's business with a plan of action in mind, a solid objective strategy
to grow their business and a SaaS-like portal to bring everything together.

Helping a prospect to visualize the opportunities for growth and success,
rather than the transactional "clear the red" approach, sets you up as the
valuable vCIO partner from the very beginning.

Onboarding Clients

The client onboarding is your golden opportunity for a great first impression on your brand-new client. More importantly, it is your best chance to show that the people who chose your firm made a smart decision. Making your client decision-makers heroes either to their bosses or employees is an often-underappreciated aspect of the onboarding process.

The way that you onboard a new client sets the tone of the entire relationship going forward. It's a sneak peek at what they can expect from you in the future.

You did a fine job convincing a decision-maker that you were the right choice as an IT partner. And even though you may have already signed a contract/agreement at this point, the real sales challenge begins now – that is, selling your team and your overall value to the entire team on the client's side.

Warning – Shameless Plug
Luckily, you've already got an ace up your sleeve to make the process smoother than it's ever been.

Of course, I'm talking about your CloudRadial digital-first client portal.

Focusing on the Purpose of Onboarding

We can break down the MSP's onboarding process into two main objectives:

1. Gather all the technical and infrastructure data you need to use during the engagement.
2. Introduce your team and processes to the client's organization.

The first objective is the more technical of the two.

It's best accomplished using a series of tools, checklists, and processes to help make it automatic and scalable. Most MSPs already have functions to do this and are adept at gathering what they need.

The second objective, on the other hand, is more in the realm of client experience. It's where your team AND your client's team gain an understanding of how to best work with each other throughout the partnership.

In both objectives, your onboarding strategy should be centered around using your client portal. Utilize it whenever possible to store and share your reports/operating information and onboarding documentation with the client's team. Be sure and include an "About our Team" section that covers the key people and processes in your business. Help you clients put faces with names of the key people they will be interacting with.

In doing so, you're already starting to make good on the promises you made when you first pitched them – things like transparency, collaboration, and accountability.

This approach unlocks a massive opportunity. Now, you're no longer focused on making the best possible impression to just the "right" people. Instead of focusing on getting the approval of the decision-makers and key technical contacts, you now have the direct means of earning the entire company's confidence, approval, and engagement.

That's a much larger number of internal advocates that strengthen your relationship with that client. It is also a potentially expanding group word-of-mouth referrers.

That's enough theory - let's divide the specifics of the onboarding process into three distinct phases.

Onboard Phase 1 – Setting Up the Company

Core Objective

- Set up the client's portal with the thing they really need during the onboarding.

Action Steps

- Set a proper feature set.

If you followed the previous chapter's steps, you'll already have the client's company created within your CloudRadial portal. If you didn't do that, go ahead, and create it now.

In either case, the feature set that you would have used for the initial proof of concept may be too overwhelming for the new company. Feature sets control the overall options available to clients and are customizable by company or groups of companies.

Figure 6 - Sample Feature Set

It's recommended to tailor the feature set to something smaller and more manageable for users as they acclimate to your portal – but still ensure that you leave on options that add value.

Keep in mind that there's a delicate balancing act here.

If you cut down your portal too much (for example, leaving just the ticketing portion on and cutting everything out), there's a good chance that the client will not see any inherent value in it, which hurts overall usage.

Conversely, a starter portal with every feature enabled may cause complexity overload – which also potentially hurts usage.

Clients will differ on what they're ready to work with. Be sure to gauge their immediate needs during the onboarding process and work to match a feature set based on what they would find most helpful.

As the relationship with them grows, you can always evolve their feature set to add new functions when they're ready.

Tailor Your Initial Content

Once you've got their company portal created with a solid feature set, it's a matter of continually refining their portal with relevant material to add value to it.

Remember that to win over the entire company and gain ongoing advocacy, you need to try and make the portal helpful to them and their business processes by making their daily lives easier.

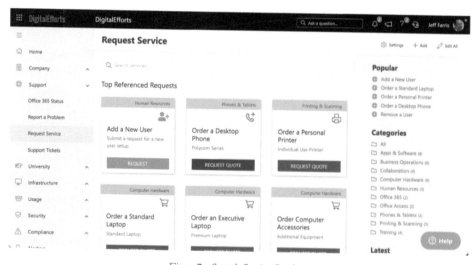

Figure 7 - Sample Service Catalog

During the onboarding phase, it's normal to use mostly sample content for the new client. Until you get to know them and their specific needs, you won't be able to finish customizing their content.

Pay special attention to these specific areas for opportunities to create helpful content:

- <u>Application Menus</u> – Links to Office 365, Gsuite or applications.
- <u>Knowledge Base</u> – An "About us" article, contact info sheet, ticket submission guide, and a ticket approvals guide.
- <u>University Courses and Quick Starts</u> – A portal navigation training course, plus any readily available company-relevant guides or handbooks in the Quick Starts.
- <u>Support Tickets and Service Requests</u> – A generalized ticket and service request catalog.
- <u>Report Archives</u> – Any report(s) with a client-facing value generated from CloudRadial or any other tool.
- <u>Assessments</u> – Any onboarding assessments necessary to gather information from the client. Remember assessments can be completed by your staff or the clients.

While the above is not an exhaustive list, it'll give you a very solid starting platform to provide the client during onboarding. Items like your knowledge base can start with introductory content and grow as you better understand the client.

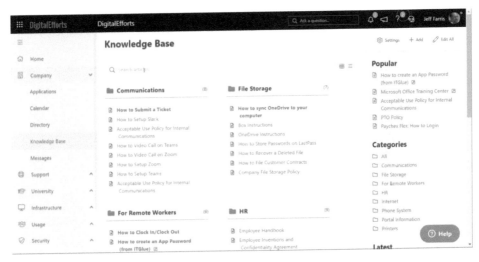

Figure 8 - Sample Knowledge Base

Make it clear to them from the start that you can accommodate and add customizations to sections in the portal as needed – be sure to make it a point during onboarding to ask for things like their line-of-business apps to add to the Applications section or for any how-to articles they'd like added to their portal.

It's recommended for you as the MSP to add the content on behalf of the client during onboarding.

However, remember that you can always give users access to create content for their organization, keeping the portal both collaborative and useful to them.

Section Recap

1. Set up a company with an appropriate feature set.
2. Customize application menus.
3. Customize knowledge base articles.
4. Customize university courses.
5. Customize tickets and service requests.
6. Customize report archives folders.
7. Customize assessment reports.

Onboard Phase 2 – Introducing and Encouraging Usage

Core Objective

- Set and enforce usage of the portal as the go-to resource for clients.

Action Steps

- Kick the portal off, officially.

Integrating the portal into daily operation is an integral part of your onboarding process. But your clients need to know that you're serious about it, too – so make sure you don't just mention it once in passing as an option to only certain people or as an add-on to your service.

If you want to see engagement across the entire organization, make sure you promote it properly. Design a launch plan, or blueprint, that you can use across clients. A sample launch plan is part of CloudRadial.

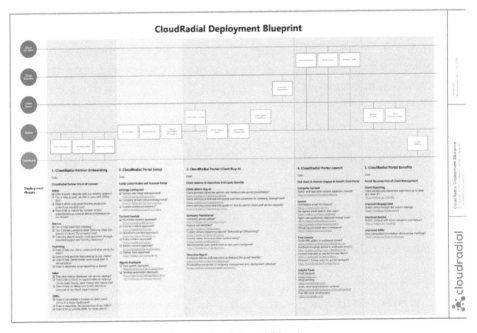

Figure 9 - Sample Launch Blueprint

That's especially true (and important) during the onboarding phase before the client has time to form any potentially bad habits.

Many MSPs complain and suffer from poorly trained clients that break processes all the time. To give an example, that's through things like improper ticket submission channels (like email, text, and phone calls) or not sticking to following operational protocols (like data deletion).

Eliminate these behaviors from the start by putting the resources they need in their portal from the get-go. Then, be sure to have an established launch that makes the portal official to the clients.

Many MSPs will host a kickoff meeting or some type of meet-and-greet onsite. A kickoff meeting is a great way to set the expectations for the organization's users and reinforce that they're just a portal away from getting their questions answered, their problems solved, and their work facilitated.

Email is another way to get your message out but remember how many emails you routinely skip over in your inbox. Being onsite or giving clients something tangible like branded coffee-mugs, pens or post-it notes helps communicate the onboarding.

Remember the strategy behind going for a mass-appeal approach to clients – you never know where additional opportunities for work and potential projects will come from.

Other than just having the day-to-day support, opening your MSP up to the entire organization also gives you the benefit of understanding each user's needs, driving your partnership to a deeper level.

Facilitate and Reward Usage and Interaction

Depending on what the new client's organization was accustomed to doing for IT support/services, driving adoption and usage of the portal may range from easy to challenging.

If they were used to a similar IT process from previous experiences, you'll notice a quicker acceptance on the portal and a smoother onboarding process overall.

Unfortunately, that's not always the case. Old habits are hard to break.

To address low acceptance and troublesome users, make sure to set rules early to enforce and reward usage of the portal and adherence to your onboarding protocols.

Remember that while adding content relevant to their organization can make a huge difference in the usage of the portal, you can always add incentives on top of that.

Some examples of incentives and procedures to consider implementing include:

Faster SLA Response Times
Tickets submitted through the portal will be resolved faster. Tickets come in with more complete information and when using preset routing can come in triaged and ready for work by the right level of technical staff. Promote this fact to users as a benefit to them. It may be faster to create a ticket by email, but it gets fixed faster when submitted through the portal.

Required Portal Procedures
For some operations, like onboarding or offboarding users, complete information is a must. Require that these requests are handled through the portal. Use CloudRadial's permalink feature to direct clients to the right forms.

Service Catalog Discounts
Promote certain hardware accessory items in the catalog at a discount. For example, showcase a wireless mouse or keyboard setup as a loss leader so that clients learn to shop for items through the catalog.

Course Completion Rewards
User training mutually benefits both the MSP and the organization, especially for training regarding software and security. Throw a client pizza party when every user completes the security training course or even a "Welcome to our MSP" course.

Section Recap
- Send pre-launch and launch emails and build a strategy around them.
- Visit onsite or deliver other items to gain visibility and promote the new relationship.
- Develop a reward system to encourage adoption of the portal.

Onboard Phase 3 – Expanding Availability and Purpose

Core Objective

- Improve the availability of your portal and reinforce its usefulness.

Action Steps

- Expand the reach of your portal through different channels.

Making the portal more available to your client is an excellent way to reduce friction with users and improve usage. The easier you can make it to access, the better.

During the onboarding phase, you're likely already performing a lot of work regarding standardizing policies and software deployments (such as your RMM software and several other potential agents).

Consider the deployment of your branded CloudRadial Windows desktop application and Microsoft Teams application at this stage to ensure that you're covering your bases from the beginning.

The desktop application can run the portal from the user's Windows PC on their desktop and system tray (which also has unique benefits compared to the web application).

Alternatively (or additionally), you can also deploy your portal out as a custom Microsoft Teams application that runs the portal natively within their Teams program. With a native auto-login function, it's a game-changing way to ensure that your MSP portal is only a click or tap away on any device and operating system that supports Teams.

This is also a perfect time to deploy out the data-gathering agent if you haven't already. Remember that this is different and separate from the desktop application and isn't interactive.

Since this information can be used for reporting purposes, which will come in handy later, pushing it out during this stage will proactively ensure that the data is already loaded within the portal.

Incorporating Communications

You'll eventually reach a point during the onboarding phase where things settle down – you've completed assessments, customized the client's applications, made sure that the ticket catalogs are suitable and functioning, and so on.

Now, you're ready to maintain engagement with some communications efforts.

One of the biggest strategic benefits you gain from having a centralized portal is having a captive audience for communications. If you've trained the client to use the portal, you now have a viable way to reach them for messages and updates on various things.

Let's take a service outage as an example.

With your portal, you can add a banner to the log-in screen, the home page, and even the ticket page to ensure that your customers are aware of the outage. A simple banner can help cut down on redundant tickets from the client while also keeping them better informed. Banners can be linked to messages for more complete information.

Figure 10 - Sample Messages

If you've deployed the desktop application, you also can push broadcast messages out that will pop-up out of their application from the system tray. That means having the ability to instantly communicate with them whenever you need.

Aside from purely practical reasons, understanding and applying these communications tactics makes sure that your client relies on the portal more and more for your updates. In turn, that improves usage.

In one centralized location, you can now set a communication strategy that scales from individual to hundreds of clients at once.

Some MSPs prefer to do this in tandem with their initial deployment, but others prefer to do so once the portal is rolled out. Consider how you've communicated with clients in the past to set the precedent with how you'll do so with the new portal.

Section Recap
- Deploy the CloudRadial data agent.
- Deploy the CloudRadial desktop application.
- Deploy the CloudRadial Microsoft Teams application.
- Set up and deploy banner notifications.
- Set up and experiment with broadcast notifications.

Your New Onboarding Process

This chapter was intended to help you build a standardized, repeatable process that is flexible enough to accommodate custom content but rigid enough to run through a checklist.

In short, the key to all of this is scalability.

It's not just for how the service team or account managers handle onboarding clients, but for the entire MSP. Putting forth the effort to onboard the client in a centralized process that revolves around your portal ends up paying off exponentially.

Once the processes and strategies are established, you have a remarkably solid bedrock to build a lasting IT foundation with your clients. And a very profitable one, at that.

Managing Clients

Efficiency in client management is a key determining factor in your profitability. But efficiency for smaller or less demanding clients often means not talking with them on a regular basis.

In a labor-first environment, efficiency is using less labor. But in a digital-first approach, efficiency is giving every client the maximum amount of online opportunity. That's why in a digital-first environment, the biggest changes you'll deliver are in this phase of the client relationship. Now, you'll be able to deliver:

- Daily QBRs automatically to every client
- Customizable content tailored around client needs
- Training and self-help resources to improve client productivity
- Additional service requests that can open new service and product opportunities
- Insights into IT assets that give clients more control

These changes make client management more scalable and less labor-intensive. You'll be able to delay hiring account managers or make the ones you already have much more productive. <u>When routine things are pushed through the portal, more time is available to elevate discussions to the vCIO level</u>. You'll see a significant quality of life improvement for your team and the client's team alike.

Defining the Scope of Management

The management phase of the client lifecycle is the culmination of several important points in your relationship with the client.

- It's where you customize the content you build for specific clients to better fit their needs.
- It's where you fully optimize your service delivery to work better with fewer resources.
- It's where you build, fine-tune, and scale your account management process and strategy.
- And perhaps most importantly, it's where you make good on what you promised the client you'd deliver when you first pitched them (transparency, collaboration, useful resources, etc.).

Let's see some practical examples of what the ongoing management of the portal looks like.

Let's break down the management phase from three distinct viewpoints – the client's perspective, your service team's perspective, and your account manager's perspective.

Ongoing Management for Clients

Core Objective
- Provide a continually evolving portal that keeps the client engaged with you.

Action Steps
- Continually evolve the portal and its content.

A big reason why people turn to having a client portal is the engagement they get with their clients. It may be tempting to quickly launch your portal as just a one-size-fits-all ticketing portal for rapid setup, but this approach most often results in low usage.

The number one thing that drives users to the portal is their perception that doing so benefits them. And these benefits need to be communicated or sold to clients. The more clients appreciate how the portal helps them, the more likely they are to turn there first. This drives client collaboration.

The more the client collaborates with the MSP and puts forth effort into the relationship, the "stickier" they become – and the deeper the partnership evolves.

You may have started clients out with generic content (such as generic ticket forms, service catalog items, and articles) to provide them with a functional starter portal as you got to know them.

But as your MSP gets more familiar with the client's work processes and needs, you've got a fantastic opportunity to keep the client's users engaged with fresh, helpful, and relevant content.

Generally speaking, the best places to add content are:

- Menu Applications – Provide new links to this area as your client's line-of-business apps change and evolve over time. Keep customizing it to make it an ever-useful intranet for new and existing users.

- University Courses – Add new training material for the client as you become more familiar with their organization and training needs. Offer to collaborate on content creation.
- Knowledge Base Articles – Create more documentation on client-specific content processes and protocols. Make a habit of posting client-specific documentation on their portal to increase usage and value of your portal.
- Support Tickets – Build additional tickets for client-specific solutions and supported systems. Tailor the support ticket catalog to make it as relevant and straightforward as possible.

As part of a review process, make sure to take the time to speak with the clients periodically to learn about any changes to their business. Aside from being a good conversation to build rapport, it'll also give you a way to gauge and ask if they need additional content created.

You can always train key contacts within an organization to add content to the portal themselves. Remember, with CloudRadial, clients can have the ability to add their own:

- Knowledge base articles
- Messages and broadcasts
- Problem reports and service requests that route to their email
- Courses
- Quick Starts
- Report archives
- Dashboards
- Assessments
- Planner items

Clients who wish to take ownership of the portal should be encouraged and rewarded to do so – especially since that both makes the portal stickier AND lessens workload on your MSP team.

Getting User Counts Correct

MSPs face the challenge of keeping track of their client's users and license counts/allocations (particularly with Office 365). The problem often exists on the client's side as well – particularly for larger organizations.

As part of the onboarding process, you've likely gained access to a base of the client's users that you've added to your PSA tool. Ideally, you've got access to their Office 365 tenant as well.

With either (or both) sources of user information, you can use the portal as a mutual user management tool in a useful and beneficial way to add value to it for both parties.

Once you've tied in their PSA and Office 365 identifiers into their company, they will sync users from both sources and create a single list that is consistent across systems. The users will be visible within both the usage area of the portal for company administrators and in the company directory area for users. This synchronization means that everyone is on the same page for active users.

Figure 11 - Sample Sync Options

With many MSPs billing by users rather than devices, a solid synchronization between Office 365 and the PSA that is visible to company management becomes critical. When users and user counts are visible at all times to clients, it is much easier to keep updated with the correct numbers for invoicing.

Getting License Counts Correct

With Office 365 connected, the client can see their license counts. Again, this keeps everyone current on which licenses belong to which users. With more transparency, issues and differences become a collaborative effort with clients.

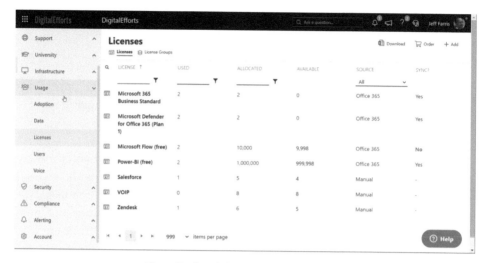

Figure 12 - Sample Office 365 License Reporting

As the relationship with the client grows, this transparent view into what you see for their organization can help both parties stay accountable to things like user provisioning, billing, cost savings, and more. Make it a habit to review and audit the user and license lists as necessary.

Learning and Adapting to Client Needs

During the initial build-out of their portal, you might have put the client on a limited feature set to simplify the roll-out as part of a "phased" approach.

Now, it's time to revisit their current feature set.

It's recommended to periodically expand out their feature set to add new menu options over time. As their relationship with the MSP and subsequent usage grows, so should their options within the portal.

Generally speaking, you'll want to start opening up more reporting and analytical sections of the feature set to set the stage for strategic discussions down the line (like client-facing assessments, dashboards, and more). But, that's not a hard and fast rule – it depends on what you prefer to show your clients.

Some clients may be happy and productive with smaller feature sets, while others may want more detail and depth of content. It simply depends on the people you're dealing with.

The client management phase is also a good time to further customize content, in addition to adding it to their portal.

For example, you may want to customize things to only show specific, custom-made user groups rather than just basic users and admins. This adds a layer of depth to the portal for more granular content distribution.

In a similar vein, you may want to add more subtle forms that speak to that client's needs. Most commonly, MSPs customize onboard/offboard forms to speak to individual client needs.

At this stage, you should be breaking off from the template whenever necessary to make these finishing touch customizations for the client's portal.

Section Recap

- Add content for the client and empower them to add their own.
- Fine-tune the sync settings and review user counts with the client.
- Upgrade the client to a more appropriate feature set, if needed.
- Further customize content to fit their specific needs where necessary.

Ongoing Management for the Service Desk

Core Objective

- Streamline the service desk's jobs from the outside-in.

Action Steps

- Optimize the collections of ticket information with questions.
- Pre-triage tickets through routing.
- Create consistency with checklists and scripts.

The CloudRadial portal is intended to be used primarily by two target audiences: The users on the client's side and the account managers on your MSP-facing side.

However, there's a "hidden" third target that should benefit from the portal – the service desk.

The service team powers ticket support, routing, and resolution. It makes a lot of sense to involve them in the conversation regarding ticket submission, especially at this phase.

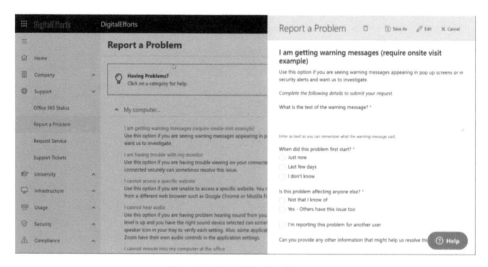

Figure 13 - Sample Problem Reports

To get your portal running quickly, it's generally recommended to use sample content wherever possible. The ticket catalog and service requests are no exception to this recommendation.

But during the management phase, you should have a bit more time to examine the client's needs and perfect their tickets. Saving time for the service desk is paramount – even a few seconds shaved off here and there can add up quickly to a ton of time saved for the MSP.

The four main areas to optimize within the tickets are:

- Questions asked within a ticket
- Routing (boards, queues, types, subtypes, source, etc.)
- Approval workflows
- Automation processes

Let's briefly run through each area.

Ask the right questions in your tickets

The questions you ask within a ticket form can make or break your support team and users alike. During the management phase, take time to comb through tickets and see if you can improve how you ask questions to resolve tickets.

The best ticket forms ask few (but very detailed) questions. Use plenty of conditional statements when you can, as well as page breaks, to make your ticket forms feel legible and easy to complete.

Make the most of your ticket routing

Equally important are the routing options you set for each ticket you create. The ones you see available to you in the tickets depend on the PSA connected to your CloudRadial portal. Certain PSAs, such as Autotask and ConnectWise, support many different customizations for each ticket.

Taking the time to go back and either create more custom ticket catalogs or to "dress up" the sample one with more routing details can pay off exponentially to decrease triage and resolution times.

Plus, the more details the tickets have within the routing info, the better the client and MSP reporting – and if you can take care of it before the ticket is even submitted, why not do so?

<u>Set up approvals when relevant</u>
Remember that your CloudRadial portal can send branded ticket approval emails to users within your client's organization. During this stage of the client's management, it's a good idea to go back and determine if you need to elect specific tickets to require this approval workflow.

These workflows can save the service team (and even the sales team) a tremendous amount of time. Not only do you get to save time by not having to chase down approvers, but you also get a formal approval process that's both repeatable and automatically enforced.

And it's not just your benefit here – the client benefits from it, too. They can potentially prevent unauthorized users from ordering things and submitting tickets.

<u>Build out your automation</u>
In the portal, the goal with ticketing is always to make the service team more efficient and scalable. The options besides questions and routing are ways to help build that automation flow out to do just that.

You've got a few options to explore in this regard:

- <u>Confirmation Messages</u> – Popular uses of confirmation messages include thank you messages, follow-up steps to tickets, and even suggested helpful resources to consume to try and fix the ticket before the service team gets in contact with them. You can also integrate appointment settings apps to book onsite or online meetings.
- <u>Checklists</u> – Checklists add a series of structured to-dos to tickets as they come into the PSA. This can be massively helpful to help scale the ticket process – if tickets come with to-dos to follow, then you can make the newest person on the service team as effective as the most experienced veteran since they're following the same steps!
- <u>PowerShell Scripts</u> – Using variables from the responses that users enter, your CloudRadial portal can also create (but not execute) a PowerShell script. This comes attached to the ticket when submitted – the theory being that a service desk person can simply take the script and run it to resolve an issue with great speed and accuracy.

These are just three examples. Additionally, each ticket can be routed to email addresses and even webhooks like Slack, Teams, and a general JSON webhook.

While these advanced automation triggers are the hardest to master, they offer the greatest potential benefits to the service team (and MSP) in the long run.

Section Recap

- Review ticket questions and routing for clients.
- Set up and test approvals wherever necessary.

Ongoing Management for the Account Managers

Core Objective
- Build a process to address the small issues before client meetings.

Action Steps
- Keep your eyes on the prize.

With all the steps covered thus far, we're fast approaching the point where the portal will run smoothly with minimal input. The clients are collaborating on the portal, the content is customized wherever necessary, and the service desk is handling the account as efficiently as possible.

But before we can launch to the final stage of the client lifecycle (growth), the account management team must first understand the bigger picture. Why should they center their strategy around the portal?

A brief look back at landing a client should help put things in perspective.

Back then, we discussed the overall goal of building a rock-solid IT foundation on which to build the relationship. The idea was to center the client's experience in a collaborative way around the portal.

That way, you can lead the partnership in a transparent manner while giving your team and the client's team the clarity to focus on game-changing opportunities that evolve their business – opportunities that will make them money, save them money, and reduce their risk.

That's the end goal that we're so close to attaining. So don't lose sight of that goal!

Your team can't think big if they get bogged down in reviewing small things. You've worked hard to set up the portal to give the client the information they need when they need it.

Now, you'll build a process to address the small issues proactively so we can focus on the big picture stuff exclusively during client meetings.

Developing a Scalable Account Management Process

The biggest strength in centering the account management process around the portal is the same thing we talked about at the beginning of this guide: scalability.

You want to build an account management process that works equally well for a one-person shop client as it does for an enterprise-level client. To do that, you need two key seemingly conflicting attributes:

- Consistency
- Flexibility

Consistency in the portal comes from the fact that all clients ultimately have the same feature set options available to them. Once an account manager builds a process to run through key areas for review, the strategy can work for any client loaded into the portal.

Flexibility in the portal comes from the fact that each client's content within their feature set can be completely different, despite having the same feature set. Tickets, report archives, policies and more can operate completely independently from one client to another.

When they come together, these two attributes make for a scalable process. Of course, your portal needs to be able to accommodate both. But what does that look like in practice?

An account manager should use the portal to review the following important areas in the feature set:

- Ticket history of open/close/waiting tickets

  Why? To look for pattern problems or outstanding issues.

- Infrastructure of the client (Endpoints, domains, servers)

  Why? To get a quick snapshot of the client's operating environment.

- Compliance policies

  Why? To spot and remediate minor trouble issues and opportunities.

- Report archives

    Why? To ensure all report-producing services are working as expected and to spot and remediate trouble issues proactively.

- Assessments

    Why? To objectively assess and measure client progress against quantitative questions.

Training an account manager to proactively check areas within a client's feature set helps standardize the process and make it tangible and trainable.

Of course, it all depends on what you have available within your specific client's feature set – but that should start you off on the right foot.

Should the account manager find any issues in any areas, they should address them via the proper methods (like opening a ticket, letting the client know, addressing the issue there and then, etc.).

Section Recap

- Get the account management team to build a proactive process (a checklist is a good start) for looking after each client.

Proving Your Value as a Partner

The portal should now serve as the center stage for the overall client experience, service desk optimization, and the account manager's client management process. At this stage, the management phase of the portal goes on for the entire length of the client's business relationship.

Before you go further – take a moment to see how far you've come.

You've built and fine-tuned a slick process designed around what matters most to both the client and your team. You're within arm's reach of fully evolving to a digital-first and client-focused process.

Now, the only thing left is the most profitable and exciting phase – the growth phase.

With everything in order, you're finally ready for collaborative partner meetings to discuss higher-level business strategy and opportunity reviews. This is where you finally get the credit for what you said that you'd deliver during your pitch back when your client was just a prospect.

To recap so far, you have:

- Promised improvements in Landing Clients.
- Set up the framework in Onboarding Clients.
- Made it possible and delivered it in Managing Clients.

Growing Clients

To understand how best to grow clients, you'll need to keep three things top of mind:

1. Clients want outcomes, not technology.
2. Clients buy products that match the outcomes they want.
3. Clients evaluate price based on the value of the outcomes.

For example, clients don't want Webroot, they want security. They don't care if Webroot is part of the solution, a logo on your website or what you pay for a license. They just don't want to worry about being a news story.

You live in a very vendor-focused environment. Datto, ConnectWise, Sophos, Webroot, CloudRadial (yes, even us), and many more try to convince you that life is better with their/our solution by your side. But this doesn't mean that they/we translate into a positive client message. Think about the iPhone. Only some parts of the phone are Apple parts. Everything you touch and that makes it work is made or assembled by someone else. But an iPhone is the outcome people want and don't care what's inside or how it goes together.

Selling Value not Markup Percentage

When selling becomes about outcomes, pricing isn't determined based on your costs. It is based on the value perceived by your client. Sometimes this value far exceeds the hard costs you'll have in the product. Sometimes the value is much less than your costs, and it will be nearly impossible to sell.

But remember, your product is more than just your hard costs. It is an accumulation of your costs, your processes and the intellectual property you put into developing and staffing those processes.

A better example of value versus price is Office 365 (or Microsoft 365 – I just can't keep up). Clients don't want Office 365, they want productivity. But they can't have productivity if Office 365 is not provisioned correctly, secured, and monitored or training and support are not available to help with issues.

The first step to capturing value is to build a product that creates an outcome that clients want. For example, with Office 365 the product an MSP can provide is "Managed Office 365" which involves several steps:

- You setup the right Microsoft 365 license for their company.
- You bundle other Microsoft licenses or 3rd party licenses for security, backup, and management.
- You apply your specialized setup process to ensure all the right options are enabled.
- You monitor that tenant daily for login alerts or problems.
- You assess licenses regularly to make sure clients are using everything they bought.
- You set up new users with the existing standards and checklist.
- You remove users following a thorough checklist.
- You monitor MFA compliance and access to the tenant.
- You document everything for client review.
- You provide the client adoption and usage reports without them learning how to navigate the Microsoft Admin portal.
- You provide additional training for end-users so they can make the most of their 365 features.
- You help them deploy Office 365 to their other workstations and mobile devices.
- You help clients diagnose problems when documents don't sync or email doesn't work.

Now you aren't selling 365; you are selling a service that includes a 365 license and, in the process, adding IP and labor to make sure it works smoothly to address your client's productivity. It's not really 365, it is now your Managed Office 365 product, and the cost is significantly more than Microsoft's price and worth every penny to the client. Because at the end of the day, they weren't buying Office 365; they were buying the productivity that 365 offers, and they wouldn't have achieved that without your approach.

In fact, almost everything you do is based on the intellectual property you develop to drive the processes that make things work for clients. Besides Office 365, other services are just as complex and process-focused:

- Onboarding employees
- Off-boarding employees
- Provisioning cloud services
- Provisioning office productivity applications
- Integrating disparate systems, including log ins
- Implementing zero-trust secure environments
- Implementing cloud-based phone systems
- Providing data governance oversight
- Providing compliance documentation and coordination with auditors
- Activating legal-hold document retention
- Designing work and data resiliency in case of limited or extended outages

Most things are now beyond the ability of most clients to comprehend. Not because they aren't capable but because they don't have time to learn about the things you know. This means that the knowledge you've built from vendors, at tradeshows, from peers and from your own efforts is more valuable than ever and needs to be highlighted in the way you grow your business.

Creating Products Around Outcomes

"Managed Services" is an outcomes-based product. Most managed services contracts address the outcome that clients don't want to deal with technology problems. And the managed services contract delivers that result. But after selling managed services, many MSPs start selling projects to capture additional value, which works but often misses the potential for additional managed recurring revenue streams. Besides the "Managed Office 365" product, MSPs can usually build out products around:

- <u>Advanced Managed Security</u> – Solving the need for some businesses and industries for advanced security requirements.
- <u>Managed Compliance</u> – Augmenting litigation support, document classification, email encryption, PII detection, documentation, and

reporting that assists with specific company and industry requirements.

- Managed Mobility – Remotely providing device support, collaboration, and security that secures BYOD and work-from-home scenarios.
- Managed Voice – Deploying cloud-based voice and video to support online meetings, webinars and phone calls from any device including work-from-home.

The keyword in all of these and future products you might create is "Managed." To deliver outcomes, it won't be enough to buy and provision a license, it will involve innovating, creating, monitoring, and hiring the right people to put in place the processes to make an outcome work reliably.

Communicating Products to Clients

It's time to talk about the cherry on top of the managed service provider (MSP) and client relationship.

I'm talking, of course, about business review meetings.

Though the core of these meetings generally revolves around the same objectives for all MSPs, their naming convention is all but standardized. You may know these as:

- Quarterly Business Reviews (QBRs)
- Technical Business Reviews (TBRs)
- Client Strategy Reviews (CSRs)
- Technical Alignment Meetings (TAMs)
- Mutual Opportunity Reviews (MORs)

…and so on. You get the idea.

For the sake of consistency (and simplicity), I'll stick to referring to them as the ever-popular "QBR" in this book. However, I'm not suggesting that they need to happen quarterly. In fact, with the daily status information provided in the portal, the QBR should change completely so its timing can change as needed.

You can use CloudRadial as a platform to vastly improve your QBR experience by framing it around a new mindset, service productization strategy, and overall operation.

Let's transform what has traditionally been a painful experience (for both you and the client) into an extremely valuable meeting that everyone looks forward to seeing on their calendar.

Laying Out the QBR's Objectives

QBRs can mean a lot of things to a lot of different people. QBR processes are noticeably fractured across the MSP space. It's made evident by how many IT service providers struggle to find the right way to deliver them and the typical lack of consistency when they are delivered. Consistency should be part of a QBR no matter who conducts the meeting or how large the client.

To help you deliver the best QBR possible, let's look at it from the bottom-up.

Let's start with why the QBR is something you even want to put effort into working on in the first place, rather than just focusing all your efforts on doing a great job with recurring service delivery.

- The QBR is where substantial revenue opportunities can be addressed and discussed.
- The QBR is where strategic discussions about client growth and the need for more projects can take place.
- And most importantly, the QBR is where the MSP ensures client retention by proving their value as both a partner and vCIO figure to the organization.

On paper, the QBR is a no-brainer – for the MSP. To be a no-brainer for clients, the meeting needs to address their concerns. It shouldn't be just an opportunity for the MSP, it should be a mutual opportunity for the MSP and the client. The MSP and the client should both look forward to it every time – but that's seldom the case. Both sides often feel pain from them and avoid them if possible.

Remember, QBRs for the sake of meetings can be big time wasters for clients unless you focus on the key questions clients always have:

1. How can you help me make money?
2. How can you help me save money?
3. How can you help me reduce risk in my business?

It's the same list of questions you probably ask of every one of your vendors too so they can't be that unexpected.

MSPs can spend a lot of time preparing for a QBR only to realize that the clients didn't appreciate (or even understand) the effort. That's painful.

But good news! You solved the problem of client focus, preparation, and scalability the moment you went digital-first.

For now, let's solve the client issue of value. QBRs often fall flat on their purpose because they're framed incorrectly to the client from the very start. Remember, client perception is everything. So, start by reviewing how you present your services to your clients in the first place.

Framing the QBR

Core Objective
- Consolidate and reinforce the strategy around how you frame services to your clients.

Action Steps
- Reframe your service offering(s) from the client's perspective.

Remember that QBR meetings will always be about the client's business and the client's objectives.

QBR meetings are NOT about pushing a "technology alignment" with your stack of services. If clients see QBRs as a sales pitch to buy more stuff, the client will quickly stop seeing any value in the meetings and avoid them like the plague.

Instead, you need to get your QBR meetings to a point where the client completely understands, anticipates, and appreciates these discussions as strategic and high-level – and that they're all about their business, not yours.

The main objective during the QBR is to help the client understand how your efforts will align with their goals to help them make money, save money, and reduce their risk.

To do that effectively, we will need to frame your services with business objectives.

Recall the hierarchy we set forth in the chapter on landing a client. It is a good way to frame the future whether you are starting from scratch or going forward with a client.

| Decision Making |
| Power BI, Big Data, AI, Data Governance |

| Collaboration |
| Line-of-Business Applications, CRM, Teams, Phone, Conferencing |

| Productivity |
| Office 365, OneNote, OneDrive |

| Compliance |
| Assessments, Policies, Audits, Documentation |

| Continuity |
| Backup, DR, Failover |

| Security |
| Antivirus, Azure AD, SIEM |

| Efficiency |
| Mobile, Workstations, Servers, Networking, Azure |

Figure 14 - IT Value Hierarchy

The logic here is straightforward. Start from the bottom with the basic items and work your way to the top with the things that have large business impacts. Taking care of the more simple, day-to-day stuff like workstation support builds the business's core on efficiency.

Once that's established, you can start to build layers of security. Then, continuity – and so on.

This continues until your IT efforts visibly improve how they operate their business and affect their entire decision-making process. And that's extremely powerful.

Framing your services around a business hierarchy has multiple benefits, such as:

- Making it easier for clients to understand difficult, potentially complex IT efforts.
- Building opportunities for projects and additional work to move up the ranks.
- Establishing a more scalable process to operate your QBRs for all types of clients.

The IT foundation process helps change how you frame your IT services from technical sales (focused on making you more money) to business drivers (focused on making your client more money).

In turn, that innately changes the client's perspective on the meeting. Now, the QBR is a valuable meeting to review mutual business opportunities and act on them as soon as they're viable.

So now, take a good, hard look at your current service offering.

Realize that you're selling so much more than just "managed services." Always think about the IT foundation and how each of your efforts fits into a more significant strategy for your clients.

Productize Your Service Offerings

Now that you've got a framework of greater business objectives in mind, it's time to build a plan to achieve those objectives using your actual IT services.

In other words, this is where you'll productize your service offerings. Turning nebulous concepts that you sell (like "managed services") into clear-cut service offerings with boundaries makes them easier to explain and utilize in strategic discussions with clients.

It helps you build a catalog of services that you can readily match with your clients' needs, removing the pain of treating each client as a special case (which is next to impossible to scale).

Productization also has benefits for your internal team. It makes it so everyone on your team has an easier time understanding what your organization sells and how they should deliver it. In turn, that makes for a more cohesive brand experience.

To productize your service offerings, focus on the following objectives:

Standardize and Brand Your Service Names

Developing branded naming conventions for services should be a no-brainer for an MSP.

In an industry where pretty much,everyone sells managed services (or managed security, managed backup, and managed whatever), there's a desperate need to stand out from one another. Especially because multiple

MSPs can theoretically offer the same service, down to the same toolset used to deliver that service.

It's not uncommon for MSPs to lament the commodity mindset of clients and then turn around and sell a generic managed services contract with service names like Bronze, Silver and Gold just like every other MSP. This is, in fact, the definition of a commodity.

> **commodity** – *something that is interchangeable with other goods of the same type.*

That's why it's important to stay far, far away from service branding approaches that rely on generic terminologies (managed services) and those that use vendor names (Sophos security).

Why? Because these are simply commodities that a client can get anywhere. Another downside is that clients can price shop to find the lowest bidder without knowing that they can be delivered completely different from one MSP to another.

Remember that clients work with you for your expertise – not for you to re-sell them vendor solutions. Your service delivery ultimately comes down to the people who deliver the services and the expertise you've built over time to deliver those solutions.

In short, rename your solutions to something that speaks to your brand and vision as a company.

That makes them impossible to compare to others while also allowing you to focus on applying them to the client's business growth.

Identify Gaps and Opportunities in Your Service Delivery

The QBR process is a fantastic opportunity to put yourself in the client's shoes objectively.

Do you offer the right services to make a business successful? Is there a gap in the services that make up your service stack that a client would need to seek elsewhere? If so, does it even make sense to add these services to your stack in the first place?

Once you shift your service approach from a technical alignment to consultative and business-focused one, you can get a clearer picture of what to improve in your service delivery.

You may find that some services you offer are too thin on benefits, while others are overstuffed with value and can be broken apart.

Lay out a theoretical path for a business and ensure that you have an idea of what it would take to grow them from start to finish. Putting your services in the context of the IT foundation can help you understand what to offer next to your clients to keep a path of growth and opportunity in front of them, 24/7.

In breaking your services out like this, you can have a much more scalable set of solutions to offer so that you can stop treating every client's solutions as special snowflakes.

Section Recap

- Make a list of all the high-level services you offer your client and review it for gaps.
- Name your service offerings to match your brand style and overall vision.

Running the QBR

Core Objective

- Develop and apply a consistent QBR process centered around CloudRadial.

Action Steps

- Build out your core planner catalog.

With a more strategic and grounded framework driving your QBR process, you're ready for action. In CloudRadial, you'll lay out the roadmap for the client using the portal's planner capability.

The planner is comprised of a simple card-based drag-and-drop interface that keeps things (such as services, projects, and general initiatives) organized within individual cards. Clicking on a card brings up an expanded view, which you can customize with as many details as you like.

Centering your QBR around the planner gives you several benefits, such as:

- Giving clients a way to see all the services that you have to offer, 24/7.
- Giving clients insight into what they're currently paying for and what they could be paying for.
- Giving clients a visual, interactive, and nontechnical roadmap that invites collaboration.

While the planner can be used in many ways, we recommend starting with a generalized service catalog.

Your first goal should be to build out a core catalog of productized services, with each service making up an individual planner card. As you build out your catalog, ensure that your services are always framed within the context of business objectives.

As you build out your planner cards, you'll see the option to add a category to them, which will color-code them appropriately to match their business objective. That helps keep you grounded for the higher-level discussion, even if things take a turn for the technical during the QBR.

Card catalogs can be pushed out to all of your client's planners. You can always create specific planner cards that only apply to individual companies later. But let's talk about why that's important:

With a core service catalog, your smallest and biggest clients can all play from the same deck of cards. Well, planner cards.

And with a consistent playing field, your QBR process becomes much more scalable.

Reinforce your Recommendations

You've worked hard to build out a solid strategy for your reactive approach – as in, a way to present clients with service planner cards and have them react to them.

Now, you've also got to deliver on more strategic value with a proactive approach.

That means using the data points you've put into the client's portal, along with your expertise, to present your rationale behind your technology recommendations.

After all, it's these recommendations that will ultimately take their business to the next level.

In our guide on Managing clients with CloudRadial, we discussed how an account manager can organize and parse a client's data within a few key areas in the portal. These areas include:

- Infrastructure information
- Compliance policies
- Report archives
- Assessments
- Dashboards

As you review these areas in CloudRadial, you'll likely discover information that can help drive better QBR discussion. You can simply click on a piece of information and look for the "Planner" button. This lets you quickly add a card (and add any notes you see fit) to the planner from nearly any area.

Now, the strategic services you're recommending are legitimized by a client's real data points.

Utilizing the information derived from the client's portal in the QBR discussion proves that you're not just putting your services on their roadmap for the sake of upselling services.

Instead, you're genuinely pointing out tangible, visible barriers that potentially hold them back from making money, saving money, and reducing their risk.

Creating this hybrid approach makes for a more engaging QBR – but there's still one more thing.

What if Client Say No?

Sometimes, despite your best efforts and presentations, clients will say no to your proposed plans.

In a QBR, the first thing to do after you get a "no" is to document it. In CloudRadial, it's easy – follow these steps for the specific card they declined:

- Select the card and edit it.
- In the card's description field, write who said no, why, and when.
- Right-click on the card and move it to Options.

The Options tab in the planner stores cards that the client doesn't need to see on the board without outright deleting them. That's especially important for two main reasons:

- You use the data to figure out who are your best clients.
- You have a clear-cut accountability trail.

Aside from business objectives and drivers, MSPs often bring up solutions and services because what they see in their client's environments is… alarming, to say the least. From massive security risks to horrendously outdated endpoints, some recommendations end up being a higher priority than others.

In these scenarios, the last thing you want is for the blame to be placed on you in the event of a failure.

Logging that your suggested remediation effort was turned down gives you a clear-cut way to point back to the portal and show the client that you did your due diligence when it was needed.

Bringing an item back to the board is as easy as right-clicking on it from the Options tab and moving it back to the board – so it's not all gloom and doom, either.

Have good conversations with your client

After you've presented your recommendations, you'll have another key opportunity.

Because the portal is designed to optimize QBR preparation and delivery, you'll soon find yourself with more "free" time during the meeting. Instead of cutting the meeting short or packing in more sales presentations, make time to discuss the client's business with them.

After all, the QBR is just a productive business discussion.

Ask questions about where they are today and where they want to be tomorrow. Other than just making for good conversation, these discussions can accomplish a few different things:

- They give you a chance to discover new projects and "hidden" initiatives.

  Many times, the client's needs won't fit perfectly within your existing service stack. If you just stick to what's available on the cards, you might just miss the bigger picture. Here's an example.

  In a conversation about upcoming business changes, you may find out that your client plans to hire 20 new people within the next month as part of an aggressive growth strategy. Though that may not fit within an existing core service card, it certainly merits being an item on the roadmap.

  You can use the QBR time to collaborate with the client and build a plan to ensure their new hires are set up correctly in every respect. You're proving to the client that you're listening to them because you're putting their own business initiatives on the planner alongside your IT recommendations.

The client can now see that the QBR isn't a meeting where you sit and pitch them on services – it's a collaboration to ensure you're doing your utmost to support them. Sometimes that's with your own recommendations. Sometimes, that's with their initiatives. Oftentimes, it's both.

And that's a meeting that they're much more likely to want to fit into their schedule.

- They help to tailor your existing plan and add flexibility to your roadmap.

  In business, circumstances can change in the blink of an eye. Planning ahead with budgets and roadmaps are all smart moves, but there should always be the ability to change the plan on the fly without causing total organizational havoc.

  Discussions with the client help re-define the roadmap timelines on a set basis so you can always shift priorities when necessary. Aside from just being useful for organizational purposes, it helps set the proper expectation to the client that you're there for their needs – it is their roadmap, after all.

- They force you to keep your service catalog relevant and useful.

  Technology changes the business landscape every single day. What's current today could be obsolete next week – and your clients rely on your guidance to keep them competitive with their IT.

Here's a question to ask yourself:

If your services don't change over time to meet your client's evolving needs, then why would the client ever see increased value in your services?

This is one of the most important reasons to conduct QBR meetings with clients.

Keeping an ear to the ground and understanding a client's needs will help strengthen the relationship with that one client and improve your entire service stack for all clients.

During a QBR, you may find that a client is suffering through a Microsoft Teams deployment that's seeing low adoption. That's your cue to put together a Team's training project to empower them. It's also your cue to think about adding a Team's training project to your standard product catalog. If one client needs help, maybe others do too.

Or, maybe the client is suffering from low employee productivity from mobile devices – and so a new mobile device management service and strategy will come to light as a fix.

As a strategic tool, the CloudRadial planner makes an excellent backdrop for these conversations.

As you discover initiatives and collaborate with your clients on ways to improve business operations, add new cards to the planner then and there using the Add function at the top-right. Be sure to experiment with adding different statuses (like Client Approved or In Progress) and some budgeting numbers to make the cards easier to read for the client.

Multiple discussions with multiple clients may lead you to discover a new market need for new solutions in general – which you'll want to add to your core solution stack, too.

Running reports and logging meeting notes

A QBR is a rich conversation that can spawn many initiatives on both sides of the table. As a best practice, you'll want to make sure that they stay as actionable as possible.

In CloudRadial, that will come down to two actions to complete on your end.

1. Run a report to snapshot where the client's portal was at the time of the QBR.

   The portal is designed to evolve with data as the client's account grows.

You'll gradually see these changes – users and endpoints will change, policies will move from red to green, planner cards will become completed initiatives, and more.

It's a good idea to snapshot the data within a client's portal in the form of an official report. At the very least, an executive report gives you a deliverable to officially present to clients. But more importantly, it gives you a way to compare growth from one time period to the next.

You can create different report types using custom report layouts and either run reports for clients or let them run them for themselves. CloudRadial will generate the reports branded with your own information.

You can either run this report before the QBR as a primer for the discussion or after the QBR as a recap of the discussion points.

2. Add your meeting notes and recommendations to the planner.

So, you've run your report and had your QBR conversation. The last thing to do is log your notes.

Within the planner, make sure to use the Meetings tab. This area lets you add notes regarding the entire meeting's outcomes and attach supporting documents (such as the report we just ran or any other report/file you'd like to run during your QBR).

The client can now see the results of each QBR meeting within the portal alongside the context of the planner and the report. Similar to the Options tab we discussed earlier, this area keeps both parties accountable for the decisions made during the meeting.

Letting the planner stand for itself

Overall, QBR meetings are a small part of your client's busy schedules. They usually won't result in instant decisions right then and there. High-pressure planning sessions that seek immediate approval for service implementation will end up getting told "no" more often than not.

So don't push for an instant answer.

One of the enormous passive benefits of having a planner integrated into your client portal is that the client can see it whenever they want – even well after the QBR meeting is over.

That gives your clients precious time to chew on the roadmap cards in their planner and visualize them to be their own ideas. As the MSP, the best you can do is bring your strategic initiatives to them and make a business case targeted towards their unique needs.

None of this can happen if you don't collaboratively approach the QBR. So, keep it collaborative the whole way through.

Section Recap

- Create a general set of planner cards from productized services.
- Look for proactive opportunity discussions during the QBR.
- Utilize the Options tab to track decline service suggestions.
- Build and run a report to keep the data in one place.

Reviewing the QBR

Core Objective

- Review QBR data for all clients to improve your MSP business operations.

Action Steps

- Run a sales matrix report for yourself

Congratulations! You now have a scalable, repeatable way to run a QBR for your clients.

As you bring your clients to the Grow stage of their lifecycle, you'll be positioned to reap one of the most significant rewards of the relationship – visibility.

You're intended to run the QBR within each client's individual planner area. However, you will want to review ALL planners at once, and you'll find consolidated reporting in the Planner section of the Partner area including client scoring.

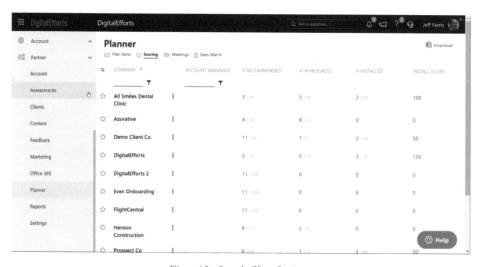

Figure 15 - Sample Client Scoring

Here, you'll get a centralized overview of the cards on every planner. That includes any card, from those coming from a pre-defined catalog to cards that were added as one-off projects during a meeting.

To keep things strategic and high-level, you'll want to focus just on your core cards.

These are the best barometers to let you know how your service delivery and stack adoption is going across your client base. Running a sales matrix report generates a clear-cut file that visually displays your clients, your services, and the status of each.

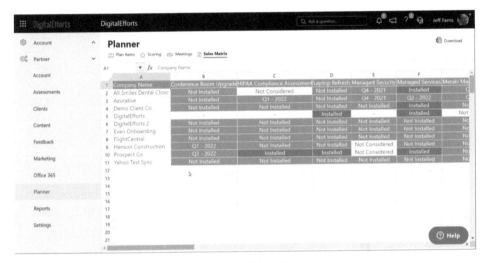

Figure 16 - Sample Sales Matrix

Running and reviewing a sales matrix shows you valuable information, like:

- Which clients don't listen to your recommendations?

  You'll quickly see which clients opt to turn your recommendations to Options. This will help you pinpoint trouble or at-risk clients and determine if you need to adjust how you present your services to them in the first place.

- Which services are getting poor adoption?

  You might have added a service to your solution stack, but you're now seeing that it's not getting traction. That should cause you to re-evaluate your pricing, value proposition, or messaging behind it. In other words, you can get quick visualizations over which services aren't landing right with clients.

Experiment with reviewing your QBR data on a regular basis, such as every 3-6 months. Doing so will allow you to get enough information to prove how your efforts are actively paying off for your MSP and your clients. When you can objectively make better changes to your service stack and value delivery, you become a much better MSP for it.

Section Recap

- Run and review a sales matrix of your client services adoption.

Co-Managing the Future

The MSP industry grew up solving a labor problem for clients. Outsourcing IT to MSPs became a way to fire existing IT staff or to avoid hiring them in the first place.

Now, the MSP industry is shifting to an outcomes-based model. The complexities of cloud operations are beyond the skills of most companies, including most internal IT departments. The MSP model no longer leads with outsourcing but instead leads with co-management.

At the enterprise level, firms like EDS, which thrived on outsourcing IT operations, have been replaced by firms like IBM, which now focuses on co-managing technology with clients. It is no longer about labor. It is now about the intellectual property that applies technology to grow businesses.

IT staffs now work routinely with MSPs to address challenges they either don't understand or don't have the right tools to address. Internal IT has become a buyer of MSP services rather than its victim.

But co-management isn't just for internal IT teams. It is for business owners as well. IT services have gone from copier-like utility to growth-enabling foundations. Well-designed IT systems enable companies to:

- Service larger geographic areas.
- Hire and utilize talent from any state or any country.
- Increase mobility without increasing risk.
- Rapidly scale up or scale down as business conditions demand.
- Transform their own products into managed recurring revenues.
- Improve decision making with better and more accessible data.
- Innovate faster with staff and clients.
- Reduce office expenses and capital outlays.

With a solid digital-first strategy and a collaborative client approach like that delivered by CloudRadial, your MSP is positioned to ride this wave of innovation and change.

About the Author

Jeff Farris is a technology entrepreneur who has founded two companies that grew globally to over 150 employees and millions in revenue. He led one of those companies to an IPO and has started or been involved with over a half dozen other companies working to establish them as leaders in their market and to successful exits.

Jeff has been involved with technology since the mid 80's, starting out with creating local area networks using Novell, IBM PC and ARCnet technologies for the Southland Corporation, the parent company of 7-11. As Manager of Office Automation at Southland, he installed and oversaw over 1,000 computers, 30 LANs, and mainframe-based email and decision support systems.

Leaving Southland in 1987, he founded Saber Software Corporation, a developer of network systems management software. Under Jeff's leadership as President and Chief Executive Officer, Saber Software ranked number 26 of Inc. Magazine's list of Fastest Growing Private Companies. Jeff led Saber Software to a successful initial public offering and positioned the company to become the industry leader for network systems management products according to IDC. Saber was acquired by Network Associates (McAfee). In the year prior to its acquisition, Saber Software achieved over $20 million in worldwide annual sales.

From IT to The Cloud

After Saber, Jeff became President & CEO at e2 Communications, a provider of hosted email marketing communications infrastructure. Jeff led e2 Communications to become the recognized technology leader with a global customer base of over 400 customers, including JC Penney,

Starbucks, Adobe, and Anheuser-Busch. e2 Communications sold in 2001 after reaching $8 million in worldwide annual sales.

In 2005, Jeff took over the technology efforts at BubbleLife.com, a hyperlocal news pioneer founded by his wife Saffie. He helped transform and scale BubbleLife from servicing one community to 250 communities nationally. BubbleLife emerged as one of the top 5 local news providers and was sold to Advice Local in 2017.

From The Cloud Back to IT

After BubbleLife, Jeff returned to his IT roots and worked with several managed services providers helping to align their business practices with new opportunities in the cloud. After seeing the frustrations of using tools not focused on the client side of IT, Jeff founded CloudRadial to create a collaborative environment where IT providers and their clients could work closely together to bring about Microsoft's vision of the modern office.

Jeff has also served on various boards of directors and assisted numerous technology startup companies. He has a Bachelor of Science in Computing and Information Sciences from Oklahoma State University.